how to go

FIND

from self-conscious

YOUR

to self-confident

SHINE

ANNA LOU WALKER

FIND YOUR SHINE

An Hachette UK Company
www.hachette.co.uk

Vie Books, an imprint of Summersdale Publishers Ltd
Part of Octopus Publishing Group Limited
Carmelite House
50 Victoria Embankment
LONDON
EC4Y 0DZ
UK

www.summersdale.com

Printed and bound in China

ISBN: 978-1-78783-637-2

Substantial discounts on bulk quantities of Summersdale books are available to corporations, professional associations and other organizations. For details contact general enquiries: telephone: +44 (0) 1243 771107 or email: enquiries@summersdale.com.

CONTENTS

INTRODUCTION

If you had to use a few words to describe yourself, what would those words be like? Would they be positive – about the skills you have, your winning personality, that cheeky smile – or would they be negative, focused on the things you don't like, or wish you could change? Everybody goes through phases of feeling self-conscious, from beauty queens and brain surgeons to rock stars and quantum physicists. Whether you struggle with your physical appearance, intelligence, confidence at work or nerves about socializing, remember that these feelings are completely normal – but that you don't have to accept them.

The next few chapters of this book will coach you from self-consciousness to self-confidence by encouraging you to think positively, embrace what makes you unique, reflect on your lifestyle choices and treat yourself with compassion. By the time you turn the last page, your spirit will be lightened, and that fire in your belly rekindled.

CHAPTER ONE:

FROM SELF-CONSCIOUS TO SELF-CONFIDENT

Picking up this book is your first step towards a happier, more confident you. As you make your way through the following pages, the inspirations they offer and the challenges they pose will help you begin your journey to a healthy, positive self-consciousness, replacing feelings of worry and negativity with confidence and joy.

*If we treated ourselves the way
we treated our best friend,
can you imagine how much
better off we would be?*

Meghan, Duchess of Sussex

IS SELF-CONSCIOUSNESS ALWAYS BAD?

All healthy adults are, to some degree, self-conscious. In itself, this emotion is not a bad thing. Being self-aware and mindful of how your behaviour comes across to other people, and how you may be affecting them, are positive traits to have. Healthy self-conscious emotions enable us to take responsibility when we make mistakes, help us to measure how people are reacting to things we say and do and allow us to take pride in our achievements. Self-conscious emotions become unhealthy when they are a symptom of low self-esteem or poor body image. Then, self-conscious thoughts can lead to feelings of depression and anxiety. This kind of self-consciousness may mean you avoid socializing, that you regularly feel embarrassment or shame, or that you speak to yourself unkindly – all habits that can prevent you from living a contented, healthy life.

WHY AM I SELF-CONSCIOUS?

What causes people to be self-conscious? The roots of low self-esteem are many and varied. Perhaps your feelings have developed recently and are connected to a new work environment, or from using social media more than usual. Maybe your feelings are more deep-rooted and go back to childhood bullying or insecurities. Dedicate time to asking yourself where your feelings of self-consciousness began. Take a moment to challenge the origins of your low self-esteem and to endeavour to rewrite your confidence story.

CHANGE THE VOICE INSIDE YOUR HEAD

You know that mean voice inside your head? The one that tells you you're not good enough? Drag superstar RuPaul would call it your "inner saboteur", and it's time to stop listening to it. Try thinking of your negative inner thoughts as coming from a character – a kind of inner pantomime villain – and practise arguing back. Use a pen and paper if you prefer and write down all the reasons that negative voice is wrong. Paying attention each time these negative thoughts appear and taking the time to disagree with them will eventually reshape your thinking pattern.

GIVE YOURSELF THE LOVE YOU GIVE TO OTHERS

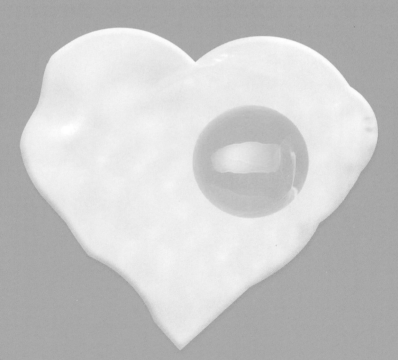

**THE FIRST THING TO DO IS BE HAPPY
WITH YOURSELF AND APPRECIATE YOUR
BODY – ONLY THEN SHOULD YOU TRY
TO CHANGE THINGS ABOUT YOURSELF.**

Adele

14

IDENTIFY YOUR TRIGGERS

Try to notice the things that trigger your sense of low self-esteem. You could use your daily diary for this, rating how strong your feelings of self-consciousness are each day. When you feel the anxious sensation rising up in you, take a moment to reflect on what has caused the feeling to flare and note that in your diary. By the end of the week you'll be able to look back and see the connections between patterns of behaviour, activities and your feelings of self-worth.

Seeing a peak when you have a social function coming up? Spend extra time focusing on building your social confidence. Feeling particularly low when you have a big presentation at work? Then improving your self-esteem at work should be the priority. You might be surprised by what triggers your feelings of self-consciousness, but highlighting the moments when these feelings are the strongest is the first step towards finding a solution.

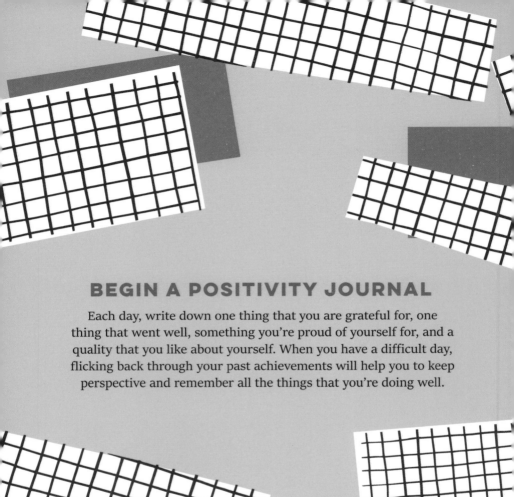

BEGIN A POSITIVITY JOURNAL

Each day, write down one thing that you are grateful for, one thing that went well, something you're proud of yourself for, and a quality that you like about yourself. When you have a difficult day, flicking back through your past achievements will help you to keep perspective and remember all the things that you're doing well.

DON'T BELIEVE EVERYTHING
YOU SEE ONLINE.
NOBODY IS POSTING
THEIR FAILURES

IF YOU CAN'T LOVE YOURSELF,

HOW IN THE HELL ARE YOU GONNA LOVE SOMEBODY ELSE?

RuPaul

CHALLENGE YOUR NARRATIVE

Keep a pen and notebook on you for the day. Each time you think of something negative about yourself, jot it down on paper. Then, when you have a quiet moment, review your list and ask yourself when these thoughts first began to enter your mind. Underneath each negative thought, list some evidence that the thought is wrong. From here, try to get into the habit of challenging damaging thoughts as they enter your head, so that you can begin to replace self-criticism with self-love.

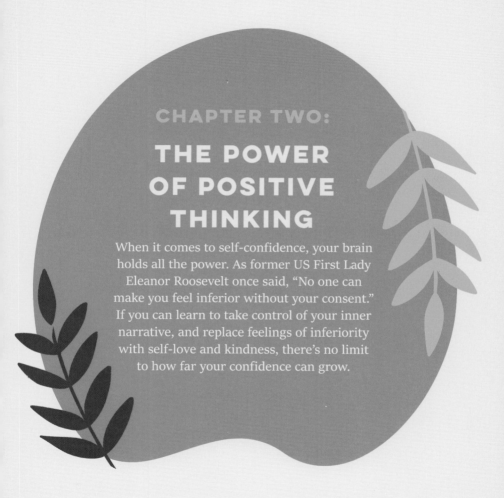

CHAPTER TWO:

THE POWER OF POSITIVE THINKING

When it comes to self-confidence, your brain holds all the power. As former US First Lady Eleanor Roosevelt once said, "No one can make you feel inferior without your consent." If you can learn to take control of your inner narrative, and replace feelings of inferiority with self-love and kindness, there's no limit to how far your confidence can grow.

TIME TO STOP SCROLLING

Our outlook can be greatly affected by social media, and spending more than five hours a day on these apps has been shown to increase symptoms of depression and low self-esteem. Take a moment to evaluate how much of your day is spent checking social media, and if need be, make plans to cut back to help keep yourself in a positive frame of mind. Most smart phones now offer ways to cap your usage, to ensure your time spent scrolling isn't having a detrimental effect on your self-confidence.

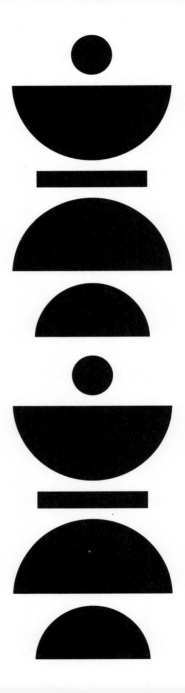

DON'T ALLOW YOUR BRAIN TO BULLY YOU

There are
always flowers
for those
who want to
see them.

Henri Matisse

IMAGINE THE BEST VERSION OF YOURSELF,

THEN BE THAT VERSION

TAKE YOURSELF ON DATES

If you don't love yourself, the chances are you simply don't know yourself well enough. Take some time out to pursue solo activities that you care about. That could mean a trip to the cinema, a manicure, visiting a gallery or sports game – any activity that you associate with joy. Invest in the experience by treating yourself to a tasty snack, or by taking a scenic walk to the destination. Start treating time with yourself the same way you would a date or lunch with a good friend – dress up nicely, be kind to yourself, and enjoy the space to reflect and experience new things. The more "you time" you allow into your life, the more you'll begin to value yourself, and think of yourself in a more positive light.

CONFIDENCE IS CONTAGIOUS

Research undertaken by the University of Konstanz in Germany has shown that high self-esteem is contagious. Studying 102 working couples over five days, they found that a person's self-esteem at bedtime was positively related to their partner's self-esteem after work that same day. When people come home from work with a spring in their step, that seems to infect their partner. Try to spend time with friends with a positive attitude and healthy self-esteem. You may just find it rubs off on you too.

STICKING UP FOR
OURSELVES IN THE SAME
WAY WE WOULD ONE
OF OUR FRIENDS IS A
HARD BUT SATISFYING
THING TO DO.

Amy Poehler

COMPARISON IS THE THIEF OF JOY

The age-old saying "comparison is the thief of joy" really is true. If you find a lot of your self-doubt stems from comparing yourself to other people, then it's time to let go. You will never know the full truth about somebody's life, or the reality behind the picture-perfect images on their social channels. Invest the time you spend comparing yourself to others into becoming the best version of *you* that you can be instead, because that's a role that nobody else can play. While you're at it, check in with yourself to see if you're also comparing yourself to "past you". Wishing you were the weight you once were? Or that you were still in your old job? It's time to stop clinging to the past, as it only slows you down. Focus on what is great about being you *right now*. I bet there's plenty you have now that "past you" was longing for.

Life can't
be sweet when
my thinking is bitter

EXPERIMENT WITH SELF-AFFIRMATIONS

You've probably heard of self-affirmations before – repeating positive statements about yourself out loud in order to boost your self-esteem. The good news is that so long as they're tailored to you, they actually work! A 2015 study published in the *Personality and Social Psychology Bulletin* found that self-affirmations will boost your confidence while also calming you down. Why not start by reading some of the statements in this book aloud? Here are some ideas to inspire you:

I AM WORTHY, JUST AS I AM.

I AM GLORIOUS AND POWERFUL.

I CHOOSE TO LOVE MYSELF.

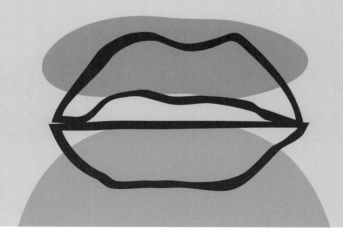

LET IT GO

It's hard to feel a strong sense of self-worth and positivity if you are still holding on to resentments from your past. Ask yourself if there is anybody in your life that you haven't forgiven, or towards whom you still harbour negative feelings. Acknowledge that holding on to these feelings creates a background level of negativity in the mind, and take the time to let go of these sentiments. This can be a difficult process, so allow yourself to take time over it. Whether you forgive somebody who has hurt you, or simply decide to let a relationship go, allowing yourself to move on from negative experiences can help to declutter your mind, and free up more mental space for loving yourself.

I breathe in positivity

I breathe out negativity

To love oneself
is the beginning
of a lifelong
romance.

Oscar Wilde

CHAPTER THREE:

CONFIDENCE COMES FROM WITHIN

Fully committing to a belief in your abilities and strengths is the key to a solid sense of self-confidence. There are many ways to achieve this, from learning new skills to stepping out of your comfort zone and unlearning the daily activities that could be holding you back.

TIME TO UNFOLLOW

Take some time out to scroll through the accounts you follow on social media and ask yourself, "Does looking at their content make me feel good?" Perhaps certain accounts make you feel inferior, that you're not doing as well as you should, or simply no longer bring you joy. Unfollow all those influencers living picture-perfect lives and replace them with accounts showcasing a diverse array of body types and interests. The more diversity you see in your feed, the less you'll hold yourself to an unrealistic standard.

YOU'RE ALWAYS WITH YOURSELF, SO YOU MIGHT AS WELL ENJOY THE COMPANY.

Diane Von Furstenberg

GET MUSICAL

Learn to play a musical instrument. A study by the University of Texas followed a group of 117 nine-year-olds in Montreal, Canada. Half were given piano lessons for three years and the other half weren't. While it didn't show any significant increase in their mathematical and communication abilities or motor skills, the children who received music lessons *did* have markedly higher self-esteem than those who didn't. So, select your weapon of choice – piano, guitar, flute, bongo drums, whatever – and invest in some courses or watch some instructional videos online. It could just be the building block for a surge of self-esteem. Not sure where to start? Beginner ukuleles can be purchased very cheaply and there's a wealth of free online tutorials out there to get you started.

YOU ARE BIGGER THAN YOUR SELF-DOUBTS

WAVE GOODBYE TO YOUR COMFORT ZONE

The next time you're at a social event, challenge yourself to leave your comfort zone by striking up conversations with people you've never met before, rather than spending the entire evening with those familiar to you. Telling new people about your life, and engaging with theirs, can make you look at yourself with a fresh pair of eyes. Plus, there's a chance you could make some new friends-for-life. There's nothing to lose!

A man cannot be comfortable without his own approval.

Mark Twain

CREATE A JOY COLLAGE

Collect some of your favourite photographs of happy moments or personal achievements and get them printed. Then, spend an evening putting together a collage or photo board of all the best images. Not only will the end product make you smile, but the process of revisiting joyful memories will remind you of all the times you've felt good about yourself, and that there are more happy times to come.

Be kind
to your
mind

YOU DESERVE TO FEEL GOOD AS HELL.

Lizzo

ACCEPT YOUR FAILURES

Start thinking of yourself as a learner in the game of life, and not as a finished product. As such, you're allowed to make mistakes, get things wrong, and be imperfect, as this is all part of your life-long education. Failures are an intrinsic part of success, and any accomplishment will be achieved with experience you gained through past mistakes. So next time you catch yourself feeling like a failure, remind yourself that this is all part of your path to success. Looking for more inspiration? Tune in to journalist Elizabeth Day's podcast *How to Fail* for celebrity takes on the importance of failure.

WHEN
THINGS CHANGE
INSIDE YOU,
THEY ALSO
CHANGE
AROUND YOU

GO WITH THE FLOW

Time to add a Sun Salutation to your morning
routine. A 2017 study published in *Frontiers in
Psychology* found that yoga poses that focus
specifically on breathing or meditation can help
boost self-esteem from within. And you don't
need to join an expensive class to feel the benefits.
There are plenty of instructional yoga videos for
beginners on YouTube if you want to give it a try.

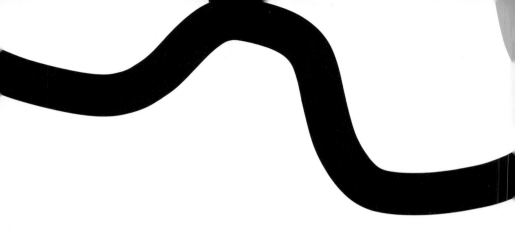

SEPARATE FACT
FROM FICTION

Try not to confuse your memory of events
with facts. Have you ever looked back at
the last party you went to and felt like you
completely embarrassed yourself? Even if
you feel that way, it doesn't mean it's true.
Our brains have a confirmation bias, which
means we tend to believe things that are
consistent with our expectations about the
world. So, if you already think that you're
embarrassing at parties, you're more likely to
believe that the last get-together you went to
was a complete disaster. Instead of dwelling
on your apprehensions, try talking to other
people who were there with you and asking
for their perspective. You may be surprised
to find they tell a completely different story!

Your self-worth is defined by you. You don't have to depend on someone telling you who you are.

Beyoncé

CHAPTER FOUR:

EMBRACE YOUR INDIVIDUALITY

If you follow the crowd, you're more likely to get lost in it. The very same traits that make you feel different and embarrassed are the traits that make you unique, and that's something to celebrate. Don't resist what makes you "you" – embrace it to release your full power.

IMAGINE HOW
PROUD
YOUR PAST SELF
WOULD BE IF
THEY COULD
SEE YOU NOW

YOU'RE NOT A SHEEP

Think about all the energy you expend trying to fit in or appear similar to those around you. Now, consider what life would be like if you stopped using your energy to blend in with the crowd, and allowed yourself to do what you really want to do. You would have so much more vigour to devote to things you care about – ambitions, hobbies, friendships. Next time you feel the pressure to conform, breathe out, relax and resist. Then put that saved energy towards something that makes you feel good.

Perfection is
the enemy of
greatness.
Embrace what
makes you
unique, even if
it makes others
uncomfortable.

Janelle Monáe

STORY OF MY LIFE

In a quiet moment, make yourself a hot drink, get comfortable and settle down to write the story of your life. This doesn't mean writing a novel – just jot down some significant moments from your childhood through to the present day. Troubles you've encountered, holidays you've taken, friendships you've made and accomplishments you've achieved. Read back through your story and you'll soon see how your unique combination of experiences have come together to turn you into the one-of-a-kind person you are today. Not happy with your life story so far? Draw strength from the fact that your story isn't finished, and, as the author of your life, you can write the next few chapters however you like.

EMBARK ON A NEW SKILL

Nothing boosts self-esteem quite like discovering a hidden talent. Think about the gifts you already have – perhaps you're artistic, or you enjoy gaming or dancing – and think about a new way to apply them. Always been into drawing? Try your hand at a pottery class. Love ballet? Experiment with street dance. Queen of shower singing? Time to book in a karaoke night. Venturing out of your comfort zone while still playing to your strengths is a great way to boost your self-esteem and maximize an opportunity to get out there and meet new people.

NOBODY IS YOU, AND THAT IS YOUR POWER

it was only until i started to be myself that the music started to flow, and people started listening.

Sam Smith

EXPRESS YOURSELF

Add more creativity into your life. Learning how to express yourself creatively is a great way to get in touch with the unique qualities that make you so special. You don't have to have a talent to feel the benefit – just taking the time to make your feelings physical is a great therapy, and to explore yourself in a productive way. Not sure where to start? You could try drawing, sculpture, writing a song, dance, photography, acting, a crafting project – the possibilities are endless.

LEARN TO LOVE YOUR FLAWS AND NOBODY CAN USE THEM AGAINST YOU

We must overcome the notion that we must be regular...

it robs you of the chance to be extraordinary.

Uta Hagen

FIND YOUR TRIBE

Happily, we live in a world that increasingly gives space to people who diverge from the traditional image of physical perfection. Whatever your insecurity, it's likely that there are now influencers who share that same "flaw" and have used it as the building block for their success. For example, supermodel Winnie Harlow's vitiligo disease has made her known as a uniquely beautiful fashion icon. There are now Instagram stars building a "skin positivity" movement posting unfiltered photographs of their acne, eczema, scars and burns. And models of all shapes and sizes are making themselves heard and taking up space in our digital landscape. Find the flaw that makes you insecure and search for a positive role model who has made it their unique selling point. Try Instagrammers @Abis_Acne for acne, @ZachMiko for body confidence or @StephanieYeboah for her take on "fat acceptance".

Love your flaws. Own your quirks.

And know that you're just as perfect

as anyone else, exactly as you are.

Ariana Grande

NEVER HOLD BACK TO MAKE SOMEBODY ELSE FEEL MORE COMFORTABLE

CHAPTER FIVE:

YOU ARE WHAT YOU EAT

The food we eat directly influences the way we feel and the ways we behave. Re-evaluating your relationship with what you consume can go a long way to influencing the way you feel about yourself and boost your self-esteem with it.

READY, STEADY, COOK!

Dust off your favourite recipe books and whip up something new for dinner. Getting creative with your meals is not only a fun way to experiment with healthier options, but it'll also boost your confidence as you master a new skill. If recipe books aren't your bag, there's a wealth of easy-to-follow cooking channels on YouTube. Try the channel "FoodWishes", where Chef John posts delicious, simple recipes all aimed at the amateur cook.

YOU CAN'T
LIVE A FULL
LIFE ON
AN EMPTY
STOMACH

You can be whatever size you are, and you can be beautiful both inside and out.

Serena Williams

SPICE UP YOUR LIFE

Keep a stash of turmeric in your kitchen cupboard. Ethnobotanists, who work with indigenous people to study native plants and their uses, have found the spice to enhance mood and combat depression, and the good news is that you can add it to almost everything. Why not try whipping up a turmeric latte next time your coffee craving comes knocking? Simply add a generous teaspoon of the spice and stir well.

THE SCIENCE
OF SUPPER

Spend some time learning about the
ways different foods can influence your
moods. Foods rich in Vitamin D, for
example, increase levels of serotonin (aka
"the happy hormone") in your body, so
eating produce rich in this (including fish,
eggs and yoghurt) can be a great boost
when your confidence is low. Meanwhile,
caffeinated drinks can lead to mood swings
and disrupted energy levels, which can
have a major impact on your confidence.
Don't underestimate the impact that the
food you put into your body is having on the
way you feel about yourself. If nothing else,
eating nothing but processed junk food will
damage your confidence because you know
that you aren't looking after yourself as well
as you should. Nourish yourself with only
the foods that make you feel good or do you
good, and you'll soon start to feel the effect.

YOUR WEIGHT MAY FLUCTUATE, BUT YOUR VALUE NEVER WILL

PLAN BEYOND THE MOMENT

When considering a food purchase, try thinking about how you will feel after you've finished eating, rather than focusing on the pleasure it will bring you while you're indulging. Wolfing down that tub of chocolate ice cream might feel wonderful in the moment, but if it will leave you with an overwhelming sense of guilt or lethargy afterwards then it's probably not worth it. That said, it's all about balance. As supermodel Gigi Hadid said, "Eat clean to stay fit, and have a burger to stay sane."

Learn
how to
treat your
vegetables
with the
love and
kindness
that they
deserve.

Antoni Porowski

THE SEEDS OF CONFIDENCE

Seeds and nuts increase the levels of both dopamine and serotonin (the hormones responsible for that happy feeling) in your body. Try snacking on some sunflower seeds, almonds or walnuts and you'll not only be eating healthily but boosting your self-esteem too.

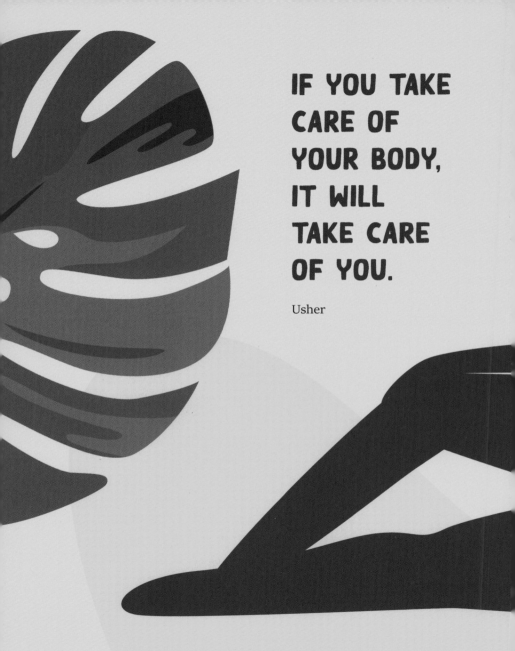

IF YOU TAKE
CARE OF
YOUR BODY,
IT WILL
TAKE CARE
OF YOU.

Usher

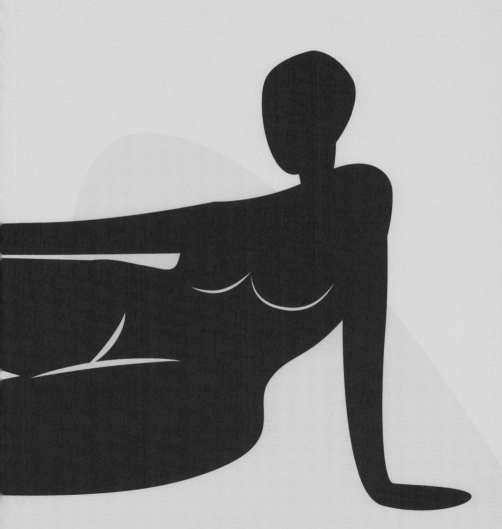

THE DOWNSIDES
OF DIETING

A report in the *British Journal of Psychiatry* found that people who regularly diet often become trapped in a vicious cycle of dieting, depression and low self-esteem. Instead of leaning on extreme regimes, or categorizing food into "good" and "bad" categories, try to approach everything in moderation. Eating a slice of cake when you're really craving it isn't the end of the world, so long as you're also eating plenty of nutritious meals. Your self-esteem will thank you way more if you cut yourself some slack and treat your cravings with balance and kindness, than if you deny yourself everything your body craves.

There is no weight limit for beauty

CHAPTER SIX:

FIND YOUR HAPPINESS HORMONES

Learning about the ways hormones influence mood can help to tighten your control over your self-esteem. Embarking on new activities like gardening, pet-sitting or exercising can all help to boost your happiness hormones and your confidence.

Happiness is a
by-product of a
life well lived

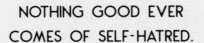

NOTHING GOOD EVER
COMES OF SELF-HATRED.

IT WILL NEVER FURTHER
YOU. IT WILL ALWAYS
HOLD YOU BACK.

Jameela Jamil

You are the
architect of
your own life.
Design it
however you
please

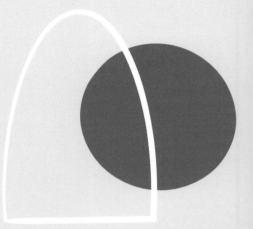

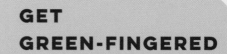

GET GREEN-FINGERED

According to a 2016 study published in the *Journal of Public Health*, gardening was shown to significantly improve self-esteem and overall mood. Consider joining a local gardening club, volunteering at a nearby allotment or watching some gardening vloggers on YouTube. And if you're short on space, try creating a mini herb garden for your kitchen window sill.

WITH HARD WORK, WITH BELIEF, WITH CONFIDENCE AND TRUST IN YOURSELF AND THOSE AROUND YOU, THERE ARE NO LIMITS.

Michael Phelps

BREAK
A SWEAT

According to the American
Psychological Association, there's
a definitive link between exercise
and mood enhancement. Just five
minutes after breaking a sweat,
you can begin to feel the self-
esteem enhancing effects of your
workout. Plus, you're never
going to regret working
out, but you *might* just
regret skipping a session.

PUMP UP THE JAM

Dedicate a few hours to creating a feel-good, confidence playlist, selecting only the songs that make you feel empowered when you listen to them. Add an inspiring photo and powerful playlist name, make sure it spans at least an hour's listening time, and voila – you have your own confidence-boosting soundtrack. Stick your playlist on when you're feeling blue, and you'll soon feel a change – it's impossible

not to feel on top of the world when Demi Lovato's *Confident* or Survivor's *Eye of the Tiger* is blasting through your speakers. Not sure what tunes should make the cut? A study by Northwestern University found that bass-heavy music was the most confidence-boosting, with Queen's *We Will Rock You*, *In Da Club* by 50 Cent and 2 Unlimited's *Get Ready For This* voted the most powerful.

DISCOVER THE JOY OF MOVEMENT

Forget about exercising purely to lose weight and try out sports and activities where you'll actually enjoy the process of using your body. Always fancied tap dancing? Grab your tap shoes and find some lessons. Secretly wishing the skater boy era hadn't passed you by? Grab a board and head to the park. You'll soon start appreciating your body for what it can *do*, not just how it looks.

To be
happy
is to let go
of what you
think your life
is supposed
to look like

I THINK BEAUTIFUL IS LIKE
LOOKING LIKE YOU TAKE
CARE OF YOURSELF.

Cardi B

FIND A FOUR-LEGGED FRIEND

According to a study published in *Frontiers in Psychology,* time spent cuddling with a pet leads to an increase in oxytocin, also known as the "love hormone". Happily, if you don't have your own furry friend you can still experience the same benefits by dog-sitting for a friend or family member. And if you don't know anyone with a pet? There are plenty of charities that offer the chance to spend time with some four-legged friends, by connecting dog walkers with elderly owners, for example. Alternatively, volunteer at your local animal shelter, for the added feel-good factor of helping animals in need.

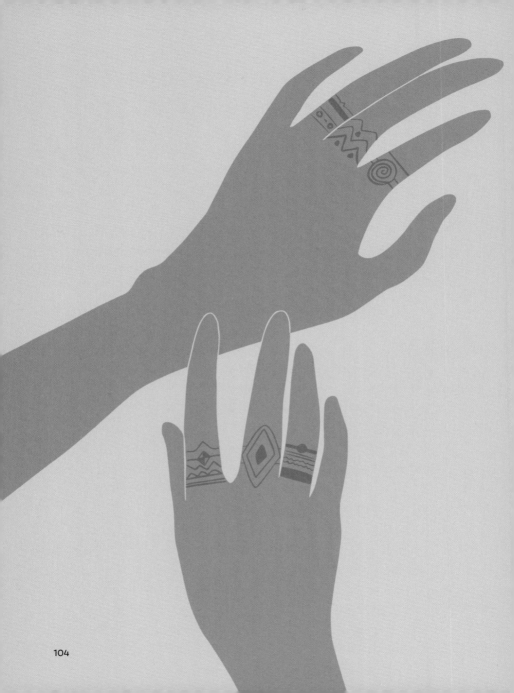

GET HANDS-ON

If you're looking for a super dose of happy
hormones, look no further than a massage.
According to a study in the *International
Journal of Neuroscience*, a massage can
boost all four of your happy hormones
(serotonin, oxytocin, dopamine and
endorphins). For a real treat, book yourself
in with a massage therapist for an indulgent
hormone boost. But you don't have to rely
on a professional. A massage from a partner
or loved one will have the same effect, but
with a bonus shot of the love hormone
oxytocin. You can even reap some of the
benefits through self-massage, so spend
some time stretching and rubbing any sore
muscles or areas of tension before bed.

Happiness is a habit
you can cultivate

CHAPTER SEVEN:

QUICK AND EASY CONFIDENCE BOOSTS

These simple suggestions are easy to carry out but could have a major impact on your self-confidence. Give one of these instant mood-boosters a try to feel an immediate lift to your self-esteem and perspective.

MAKE AN IMPRESSION

Feeling intimidated by a big presentation at work, or a scary social event? Take it back to the 1980s and experiment with power dressing. Wearing a structured jacket, formal trousers, a bold print or colour are all things that can help you to stand taller and make an impact, even when you feel like shrinking into the shadows.

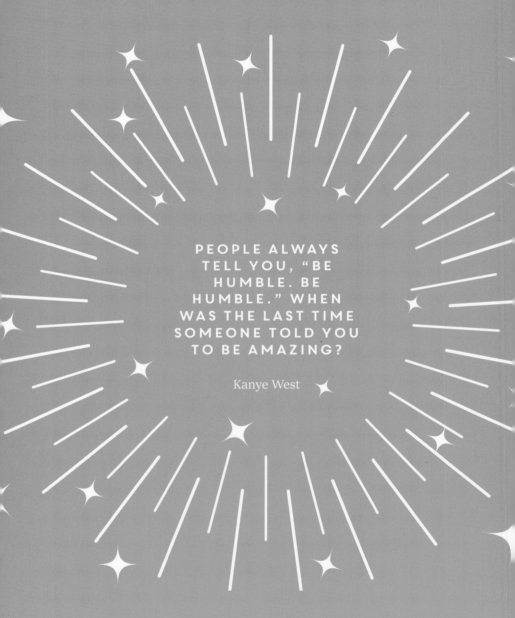

PEOPLE ALWAYS TELL YOU, "BE HUMBLE. BE HUMBLE." WHEN WAS THE LAST TIME SOMEONE TOLD YOU TO BE AMAZING?

Kanye West

STRIKE A POWER POSE

According to a study conducted by psychologist Albert Mehrabian in the 1950s, 7 per cent of the impact you have on a stranger is down to the words you use, 38 per cent is in your tone of voice, and a whopping 55 per cent comes from your body language. Take the time to stand in front of the mirror and practise your posture. Imagine you're drawing a straight line from your feet up to the top of your head. Shoulders back, hips forward, chin up – and instantly you're exuding a confidence that's hard not to buy into.

DISCOVER THE POWER OF "NO"

If it's difficult to summon the confidence to assert yourself, you may often find you're saying "yes", and agreeing to things you don't want to do. There's then a risk that you will be taking on extra burdens that take a toll on your mental health, or that you're giving in to peer pressure that further affects your sense of self-image. The next time somebody asks you to do something that you really don't want to do, forget trying to placate them or win their good opinion and just say, "no". This habit gets easier with practice and will free you up to spend your days doing only the things you have decided are right for you.

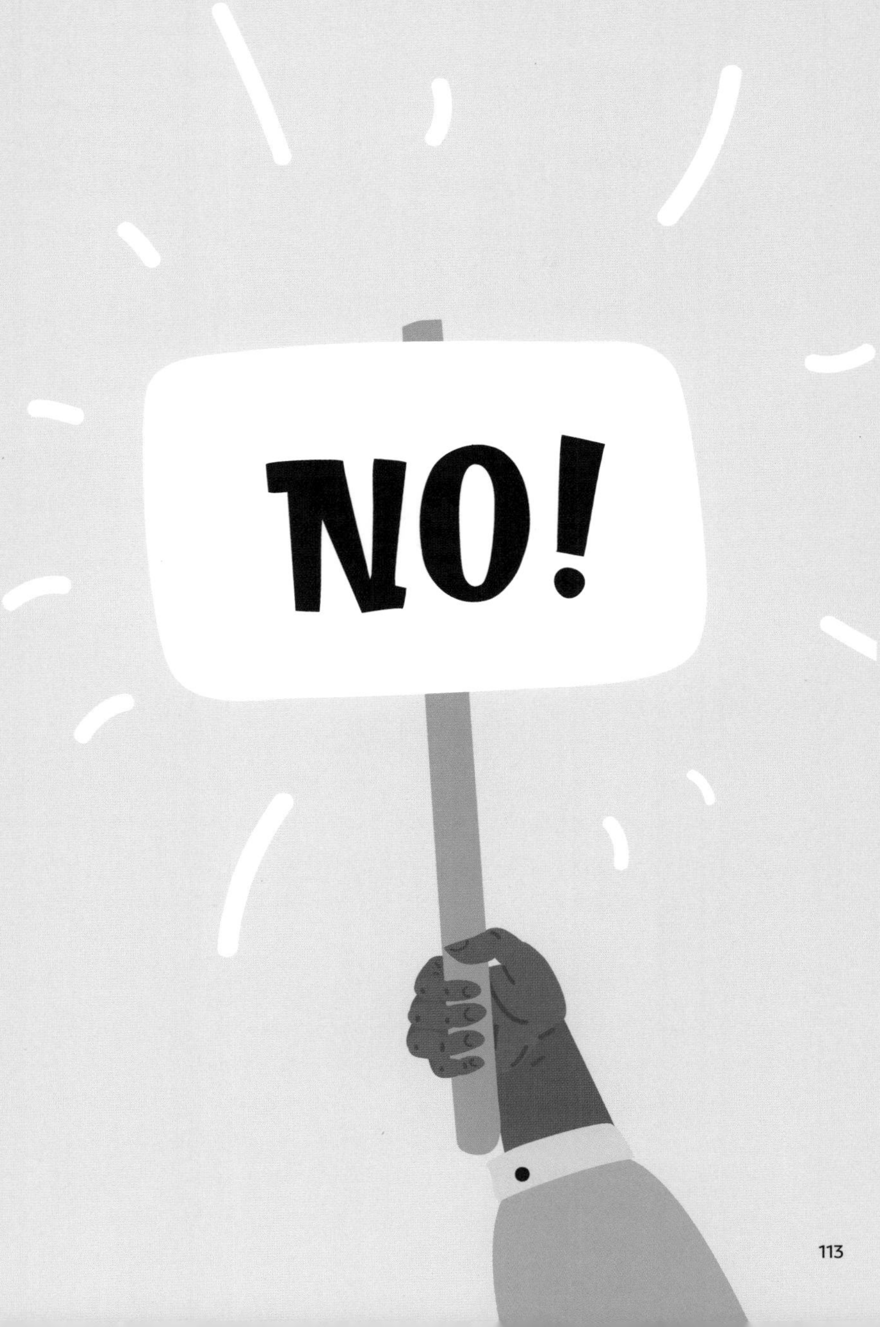
NO!

You don't need to change to deserve love

Love yourself first and everything else falls into line.

Lucille Ball

MIRROR, MIRROR

Stand in front of your mirror with a pen and paper. You may be used to using your mirror to criticize yourself, but now your task is to list five things you like about your physical appearance. Then, while still standing before the mirror, list five non-physical things that you like about yourself. Keep your list and look at it in moments of self-doubt. Consistently focusing on what you like about yourself in moments of self-criticism can help to shift your mindset. Struggling to complete your list? Asked a trusted close friend or loved one. You might just be surprised by what they say. And if you still dislike what you see reflected back to you? Move your mirror to the most tranquil part of your home, drape some fairy lights around it, and add a positive phrase or two to the frame using sticky notes or colourful paper. Seeing yourself surrounded by positivity might just change your mindset.

YOU ARE WHAT YOU WATCH

Studies undertaken by the Mental Health Foundation have found that 24 per cent of body image issues in young people stem from watching reality television shows. Be mindful of your cultural intake and the effect it's having on your mood and self-confidence. If you find that you're constantly comparing yourself to the people on your screen, it's time to change the channel.

BE GENTLE; BE KIND; FORGIVE YOURSELF

CONFIDENT CHAT

Your voice and your sense of inner confidence are intimately connected. Pay attention to your patterns of speech and listen for evidence of self-doubt. A particularly common example is using the question inflection for statements, which means your voice rises up at the end of your sentence. For example, saying, "I've worked here for five years?" Going down at the end of a sentence suggests confidence and authority: "I've worked here for five years." Hearing yourself speak with a more confident tone will affirm a stronger sense of self-worth.

I AM THE GREATEST.
I SAID THAT EVEN BEFORE
I KNEW I WAS.

Muhammad Ali

FIND A ROLE MODEL

Seek out role models who are of the same age,
gender, race and/or professional background as
you and learn more about them. Perhaps they've
written a book you could read, presented a TED
Talk you could watch, or they post about their
career on Twitter. As the saying goes, you can't
be what you can't see. Having a relatable role
model to look up to can help enormously when
it comes to self-confidence and self-belief.

HAVE THE
COURAGE
TO TRY
SOMETHING
NEW – EVERY
EXPERT
WAS ONCE
A BEGINNER

CARRY A LUCKY CHARM

In 2010, the *Psychological Science Journal* found that people who carry lucky charms with them were generally more confident going into certain situations than those who didn't, and that confidence was also found to boost their overall performance in those situations. Finding yourself a lucky talisman could become a new source of confidence, giving you something to hold on to in moments when you feel insecure. It doesn't have to be a traditional four-leaf clover or rabbit foot – anything can work as your lucky charm! The best choices tend to have a degree of sentimental value and are small enough to hold in a pocket.

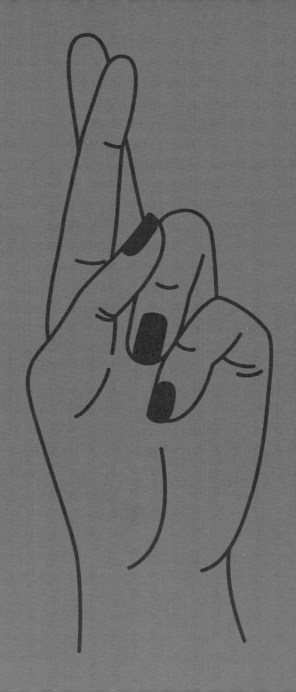

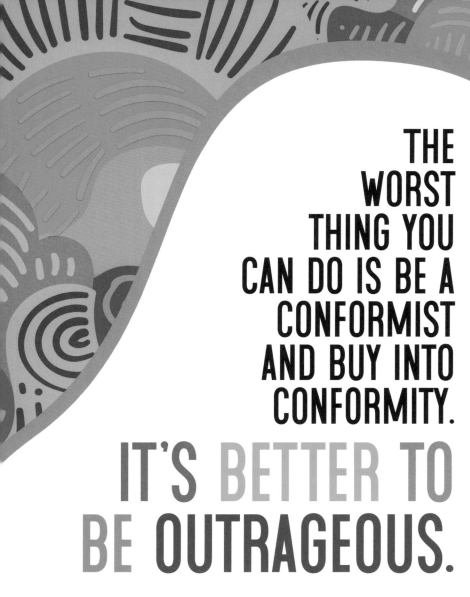

THE
WORST
THING YOU
CAN DO IS BE A
CONFORMIST
AND BUY INTO
CONFORMITY.
IT'S BETTER TO
BE OUTRAGEOUS.

Deepak Chopra

CHAPTER EIGHT:

(RE)TREAT YOURSELF

The way you take care of yourself reveals how you feel about yourself. Taking the time for some self-care, to relax and pamper yourself, goes a long way to reminding you that you have value and are worth taking care of.

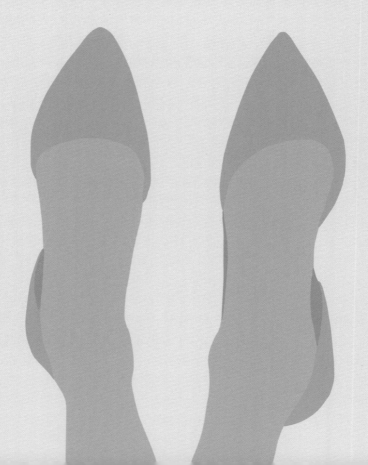

SPRITZ YOURSELF HAPPY

Make a beeline for your nearest fragrance counter – a 2011 study published in the *Neurobiology of Sensation and Reward Journal* found that a whopping 90 per cent of women instantly felt more confident after spritzing perfume, compared to those who didn't. Perfumes tend to smell different on different people. Why not grab some samples, and test them out for a few days, before deciding on your signature scent?

Try and only be kind to yourself today. Love yourself like you're your own mother.

Amy Schumer

SOAK IN SELF-CONFIDENCE

When we have low self-esteem, we often forget to take proper care of ourselves. A long bath is a great way to reconnect with your sense of self, and spend time unwinding from the pressures of your everyday life. Drizzle in some essential oils, light some candles and open up a book you can really get lost in. Then settle in for a long, relaxing soak. As you're blissing out, remember that bathing has been found to improve blood flow and immunity, relax sore muscles and joints, calm your nervous system and improve your lung capacity and oxygen intake.

133

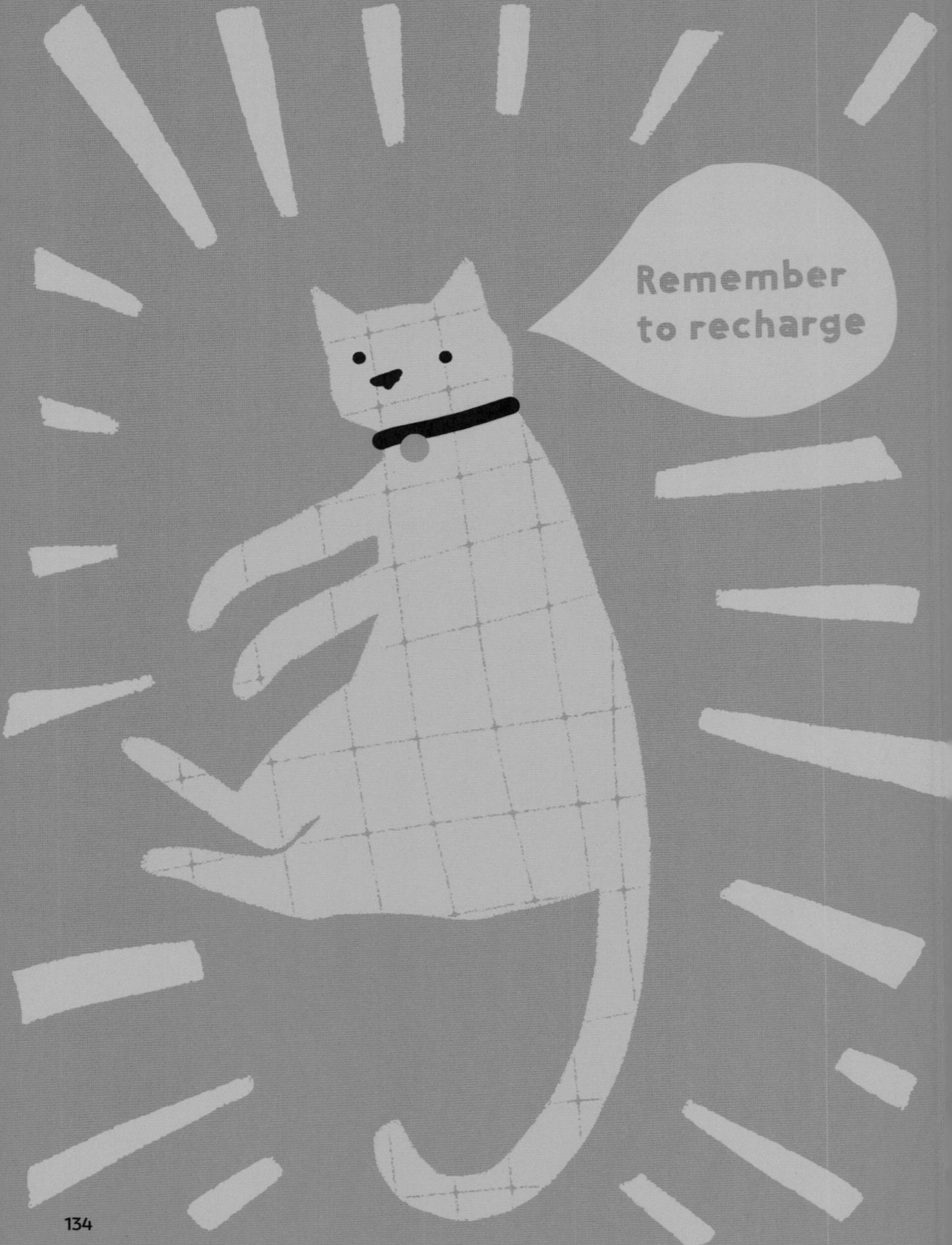
Remember
to recharge

CLEAR OUT YOUR BEDROOM

There's no better sense of a fresh start than clearing your room of unneeded clutter and turning it into a more tranquil, calming space. Hanging on to a hoard of clothes that no longer fit you? It's time to say goodbye. Take them to a charity shop or sell them online – they're only reinforcing the idea that your current self isn't good enough. Light some candles, arrange some soft lighting, and make sure that you can end each day in a space that makes you feel *good*.

Tell yourself you're
beautiful daily.
Be gentle with
yourself...
life is too short
to worry about
what others
think!

Demi Lovato

THE GREATEST
INVESTMENT YOU
CAN MAKE IS
IN YOURSELF

You have to create little pockets of joy in your life to take care of yourself.

Jonathan Van Ness

WALK IT OFF

Take yourself for a long walk surrounded by nature, especially on a sunny day. Not only will this alone time help to clear your mind and clarify your thoughts, but the Vitamin D you gain from the sun will lower your blood pressure, reduce stress and combat a low mood. It doesn't matter where you go – whether you stroll in a local park, around your town or in the great outdoors you will feel the benefits of fresh air, sunshine and movement.

SLUMBER IN STYLE

Set yourself the goal of taking an early night,
just for the pure enjoyment of it. Earlier in the
day, prepare your bed with some fresh sheets. As the
evening comes, unwind slowly with a cup of cocoa,
take a warm shower using your favourite products
and spend some time meditating or doing gentle yoga.
Then put on a clean pair of pyjamas, fall into bed and
spend your last stretch of time curled up with a good
book, resisting the urge to check any screens for at
least an hour before you hit the hay. You'll wake
up feeling rested and rejuvenated with a
newfound strength to face the day ahead.

NEVER
APOLOGIZE
FOR THE SPACE
YOU TAKE UP

IN THE MORNING WHEN YOU
WAKE UP, DO YOUR STRETCHING,
WASH, AND DO YOUR AFFIRMATION
THANKING THE UNIVERSE
FOR WHAT YOU/WE HAVE.

Yoko Ono

Treat
yourself
like
somebody
you love

CHAPTER NINE:

NEXT STEPS

It's crucial that when you finish this book, you
endeavour to change your routine for the better.
Follow these tips to create a happier, healthier self-
consciousness that will stand the test of time.

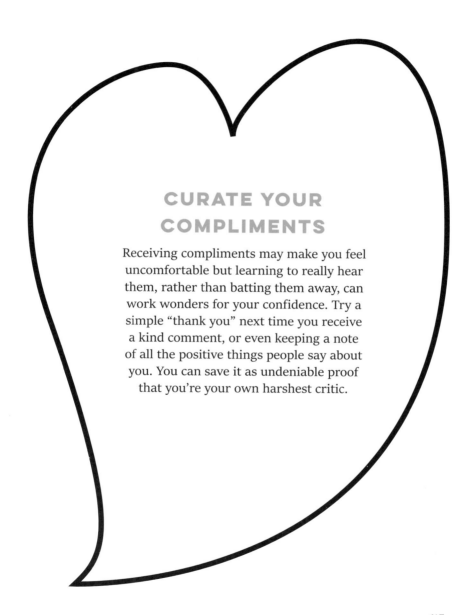

CURATE YOUR COMPLIMENTS

Receiving compliments may make you feel uncomfortable but learning to really hear them, rather than batting them away, can work wonders for your confidence. Try a simple "thank you" next time you receive a kind comment, or even keeping a note of all the positive things people say about you. You can save it as undeniable proof that you're your own harshest critic.

WE NEED TO DO
A BETTER JOB OF
PUTTING OURSELVES
HIGHER ON OUR OWN
"TO DO" LISTS.

Michelle Obama

BE ON
YOUR
OWN
SIDE

PUT AN END TO PROCRASTINATING

We all have that one chore that's been lurking at the bottom of our to-do lists for longer than we care to remember. If you only do one thing today, make it that chore. Procrastinating, even over something small, is an easy way to make yourself feel bad. Prioritize it today and you'll find that you go to bed feeling a lot better about yourself – plus you're sure to discover that the chore you'd put off wasn't nearly as demanding as you feared. From now on, stick to a new rule: if a chore takes ten minutes or less, just do it right away. The longer you put little tasks off, the bigger they seem to become.

KICK THE HABIT

Pick out a habit that consistently leaves you feeling bad about yourself, such as smoking, always being late or biting your nails. Make changing that one behaviour your focus for a month. Track your progress using a bullet journal or try the free Android and iOS app "Habit Tracker". The app allows you to set customizable goals, including adding motivational messages to your reminders and a time frame for breaking your habit. You'll be amazed at the lift to your self-esteem that can be achieved by alleviating one bad habit.

FIND OUT WHO YOU ARE AND DO IT ON PURPOSE.

Dolly Parton

RANDOM ACTS
OF KINDNESS

A study published in the *Journal of Adolescence* found that altruistic behaviours raised levels of self-worth, so try adding a few random acts of kindness into your daily routine to boost yours. It's crucial that your acts of altruism aren't only limited to friends and family. Those who helped strangers during the study showed increased self-worth one year later. This may be because helping a stranger is more challenging than helping a friend, leaving you with a greater sense of achievement.

BE YOURSELF – NOBODY CAN SAY
YOU'RE DOING THAT WRONG

IT'S OKAY TO ASK FOR HELP

If your sense of low self-esteem or self-consciousness feels overwhelming, then it's time to ask for help. Opening up to loved ones is a good place to start, as their support will be crucial to getting yourself back on track. It's also worth speaking to your doctor, who may be able to point you towards therapy options such as CBT (cognitive behavioural therapy), which takes a practical approach to solving emotional issues. If you don't feel ready to share with people around you, there are plenty of charities who can offer advice and guidance. These charities often have helplines you can phone if you'd like to speak to someone, or ways to chat online if you'd prefer. Remember, communication is the first step towards feeling better.

CONCLUSION

By finishing this book, you've already made a declaration to yourself that you're ready to invest in self-love and build your confidence. Congratulations! Hopefully you've been able to reflect on the unique qualities which make you such a special person, and start your journey towards loving yourself, just the way you are.

By making tweaks to your lifestyle – the food that you eat, acts of self-care, getting exercise and speaking kindly to yourself – you'll be building the foundation blocks of a happy, confident life. And remember, actions speak louder than words! If you behave like a happy, confident person, you'll soon see yourself become one.

IMAGE CREDITS

If you're interested in finding out more
about our books, find us on Facebook at
Summersdale Publishers and follow
us on Twitter at **@Summersdale**.

www.summersdale.com